Heaven from Steam

Heaven
from
Steam

POEMS BY
Carol Light

ABLE MUSE PRESS

Able Muse Press

www.ablemusepress.com

Printed in the United States of America

Library of Congress Control Number: 2013932426

ISBN 978-1-927409-18-3 (paperback)
ISBN 978-1-927409-19-0 (digital)

Cover image: "San Francesco a Ripa (cupola)" by Jennifer Wilkin Penick

Cover & book design by Alexander Pepple

Able Muse Press is an imprint of *Able Muse:* A Review of Poetry, Prose & Art—at www.ablemuse.com

Able Muse Press
467 Saratoga Avenue #602
San Jose, CA 95129

for RK

Acknowledgments

I am grateful to the editors of the following journals where many of these poems originally appeared, sometimes in earlier versions.

32 Poems: "Downdraft."

Future Cycle Poetry: "The Archaic Torso of Apollo."

Jack Straw Anthology: "Antoinette," "Finger Exercises," "Alba," "Cento: Note to Self," "Letter to Santa."

Literary Bohemian: "Long Distances *(With Camel),*" "Prairie Sure."

Lvng: "Hertzsprung-Russell."

Mare Nostrum: "A Cavallini Annunciation," "Doth the Same Tale Repeat," "Triads," "Met·a·mor·pho·sis."

Narrative Magazine: "Long Division," "Anniversary," "Sanguine," "Raynaud's Weather."

Pacific Poetry Project: "First Chantey."

Poetry Northwest: "Postcards from Ponza, the Prison Island," "Crossing Hood Canal," "January Walk."

Port Townsend Leader: "Long Distances *(With Weathervane).*"

Prairie Schooner: "Lullaby Postmodern," "It's Not the Heat."

Thanks to editor Ted Kooser for selecting "Prairie Sure" for republication in *American Life in Poetry*.

I am grateful to the Poetry Society of America for the 2013 Robert H. Winner Award, the Artist Trust Foundation for the 2011 GAP award, the 2012 Jack Straw Writer's Program for a community of fellows, and Able Muse Press.

I am indebted to many others who have guided this book into being. Thanks to Alex Pepple and these astute and generous readers: Linda Bierds, Cody Walker, Jason Whitmarsh, Brad Leithauser, and Kevin Craft. Thanks to family (near and far) for encouragement and inspiration, especially Maeve, Will, Hollis, and *Sorella* Susie Frazier. Most of all, I am grateful (with buss and boutonniere) to Richard Kenney for twenty years of poems and conversation.

Foreword

The poet May Swenson once observed, in a little poem called "Almanac" that was in part a tribute to Einstein, that "there is no hitching post" to the universe. True enough, I suppose, but in the alternative universe of literary creation it seems fair to say that a first book of poems is indeed a kind of stationary hub in a shifting cosmos. Where the poet will next venture is anybody's guess, but whether his or her second book wanders a short or a great distance from the first, whether the style and sounds and strategies of rhetoric will henceforth vary little or a lot, readers will regard that first book as a settled compass point. It will be a Polaris, around which later books, like the footloose other stars of the Little Dipper, pivot.

What are the fixed aspects of Carol Light's first book, *Heaven from Steam?* What's most striking to me is the way rhyme propels the poems. In declaring this, I risk encouraging at least two misunderstandings, which I'd better correct at the outset. Rhyme is commonly perceived as an old-fashioned tool, partly because the contemporary poet who embraces it often works with highly traditional forms and sounds; but this is hardly the case here. Likewise, to be rhyme propelled may suggest a high incidence of forced rhyme—the poet's thinking being channeled and constrained by long-established rhyme-pairings. Again, this doesn't apply to Carol Light.

Indeed, a casual reader could look right past the centrality of rhyme in the book's construction. It's only a small portion of the rhyming that is "clean" or "perfect" and that lands in the slot habitually reserved for it: the last word of a line. Here and there, for purposes of emphasis or change-up, Light does take up a meter and a rhythm Pope would have felt at home with, as in the closing couplet of "Long Division":

> She feather-dusts the furniture and kneads
> the bread dough with her fists. And if they'd tried
> harder? She kept the dog, but the dog died.

But far more typical is "Downdraft," which I'm tempted to say is written in blank verse, except that blank verse doesn't rhyme and "Downdraft" is, internally, a callithump of rhymes:

> And a crow
> plucks lumps of pumpkin from the compost bin.
> I dry my boots beside the fire. I set
> my tea to steep on the ledge. The dog's asleep
> beneath my elbow. Warm as toast and snug,
> smug as some tweedy squire, I survey
> the possibilities.

I'm reminded here, too, of Swenson, whose infatuation with rhyme was tempered only by an aversion to using it in expected ways and places. The second stanza of Light's "Signs" is a sonnet with a conventional rhyme scheme—except that every rhyme's an off-rhyme.

The musical challenge and delight when everything is "off" begins in the need for wilder harmonies, for something "off off" to play up against the "off." Looking for unexpected pairings, the poet ransacks the rucksack, and in *Heaven from Steam* we enter a wanton auditory domain where *sauvignons* couples with *violins*, and *business* with *isthmus,* and *dream* with *extremis* and *clamor* with *or am.*

The book is marked by a lightness of touch. The overall effect of much of the rhyming is playful, even antic. The pawky ghosts of Lewis Carroll and Edward Lear may be seen flitting through "Finger Exercises":

> Bleary tourist orders double
> jet-lag stalling macchiato,
> pays for peaches, steps staccato
> off to gawk at ancient rubble.

Heaven from Steam is an unusual first book in its avoidance of that portentous heaviness that new poets often don—like scuba drivers strapping on a weight belt—when announcing their presence.

For a first book it's unusual, too, in containing so little autobiography. My guess is that a reader new to these poems and this author would eventually compose a portrait of a woman who has a husband and a child; who has a keen eye for the natural world; who sometimes has sleep problems and finds inspiration in inclement weather. But our reader would still be a long way from being able to fill in the blanks on Light's CV.

Still, such a reader would probably conclude that Light has three "special places"—wellsprings where she regularly goes dipping for inspiration: the Pacific Northwest, Italy (particularly Rome), and the Prairie States. I wish there were more poems about the last of these places, which she captures quite hauntingly:

> The leaning gossip, the half-alive ripple
> of sunflowers, sagging eternities of corn
> and sorghum, September preaching yellow, yellow
> in all directions, the windowsills swelling
> with Mason jars. . . .
> . . .

> The dust, the heat, distrusted, the screen door
> slapping as the slat-backed porch swing sighs,
> the hatch of houseflies, the furlongs of freight trains. . . .
> ("Prairie Sure")

That's a wondrous final line. With "the hatch of houseflies" we find ourselves in many senses in an earthbound world—a place of decay and foulness and annoyance and circling, incessant repetition. But "the furlongs of freight trains" transports us to another place entirely. That odd, antiquated, venturesome *furlongs* evokes all the romance and sweet promise of travel; its second syllable sings of *longing* housed within those shuddering boxcars.

I've emphasized Light's lightness, so to speak, but she strikes another tone entirely in the crowning sonnet sequence, *"Vicolo del Divino Amore."* As the poem unfolds, I wasn't surprised at the nimbleness with which she weaves and unweaves her lines and imagery around the birth of a yearned-for child. But I wasn't fully prepared for the surfacing of an august yet plainspoken grandeur, delivered without self-protective irony or self-questioning qualification:

> At night, sometimes, when I forget
> to breathe, asleep, I find myself—some aspect
> of myself—caught between the depths and shoals
> of dream and reason. When the tide is calm,
> I preach the gospel of observation.

And there's a bold and gorgeous stretch of lines in praise of physical consummation:

> The soul applauds,
> the body's bell resonates—the tone marching
> from toe to ear, from lip to fingertip.
> And we are safe in the beloved's arms,

to go beyond, where pleasure knows no peril,
where all is easy alchemy, hip to hip.
No fall from paradise. The carnal charm—
when flesh, blessed, spent, rung, still peals the carillon.

Lines like these are a reminder that, of all the traditional poetic virtues, stateliness may be the one that in our time we're least comfortable applauding and pursuing—our loss, of course. For this reason, and a host of others, the appearance of *Heaven from Steam* is a welcome sight.

—Brad Leithauser

Contents

WINGED ELBOW

VICOLO

Heaven from Steam

WEATHER

Crossing Hood Canal

And is there really rescue in the wind?
A helicopter knifes the sky above
the far end of the bridge. Below: cones,
striped barricades, one blue patrol car.
Leaning against the Taurus, there he is:
the predictably square-jawed trooper masked
in silver aviator frames. He's dressed
and ready to escort you to a less
venial detention. Twitching, you pass
the mirrored lenses cautiously by. Dismissed,
you begin your slow ascent. The faintest star
winks just after sunset. Atonement postponed,
you're not the body sought at all, cream puff,
and, knock wood, neither are you dead.

Signs

Danger. Do Not Enter. The path to the beach
is cordoned off. Two scofflaws duck below
the caution tape and clamber over blown-
down trees and gale-split snags; late gusts reach
for weak limbs, yet. A dory slips her mooring
and chafes against the rocks. Fine weather
for nooses, suggests the rope, dangling in water.
An orange cat yawns from a porch. Early this morning:
flame-licked windows, a living room catching fire,
a woman who sweeps herself into a corner,
weeping for singed hair. Time to call the coroner?
What extinguisher will wash the mind of fear?
The oblivious Dalmatian sniffs at the base
of the streetlamp. We know we are not safe.

Signs say so. A crow fastens itself
like a hood ornament to conversation. I resist
the day's bright-unbuckled smiles. The Irish
scrape soil from crevices, as I do. *Selfish,
what a shellfish you are,* the gulls chuckle, flapping
like bedsheets above. An eagle glides low over
the lock-kneed couple. Walking, they are lovers,
unaccustomed to flailing. They are blasphemers
admiring his marvelous wings. The feathered quorum
riding the bell buoy deafens to its changeless
chime. No wisdom comes from ancient sages;
true voices sing to us from the children's choir.
We give ourselves daily to the god of the winds to be torn.
Surprised, he gives back to us this generous storm.

Prairie Sure

Would I miss the way a breeze dimples
the butter-colored curtains on Sunday mornings,
or nights gnashed by cicadas and thunderstorms?
The leaning gossip, the half-alive ripple
of sunflowers, sagging eternities of corn
and sorghum, September preaching yellow, yellow
in all directions, the windowsills swelling
with mason jars, the blue sky bluest borne
through tinted glass above the milled grains?
The dust, the heat, distrusted, the screen door
slapping as the slat-backed porch swing sighs,
the hatch of houseflies, the furlongs of freight trains,
and how they sing this routine, *so sure, so sure*—
the rote grace of every tempered life?

Raynaud's Weather

i.

So, what did I expect? Not this: March snow
flung slant-wise, rice-like, from a glowering sky.
Here at the bakery, one dapper groom
waits for his bride atop a three-tiered cake.
The damp camps outside, clouding the mind. Chapped
lips breathing through my ungloved knuckles, I try
to thaw these bloodless fingers. A heart will take
precautions, withholding warmth, but it's mistaken.
What's just around the corner? *Spare me.* Tires
slam the curbside puddles, splashing the matted
leaves where faithless grass lacks the naked
nerve to grow. A cold gust lifts the grim
tulle veil, a flash of blue! But the gods deny
this kiss, returning mist, spring in escrow.

ii.

Budless oak branches
card a woolly sky. Sleet spits
at green junipers.

They needle no one.
Does the cardinal never
complain of the cold?

No vitriol from
the vireo. An ice square
glares from the brown lawn

where the child's snow fort
once stood. Whatever happened
to stoicism?

Bleating heart, buck up.
What did you expect? Not March.
Note: send daffodils.

It's Not the Heat

It's the bikinis simmering
with sun worshippers;
they freckle the sand
and convertibles crawl the streets,
ogling beach bronzes,
the loud bass line swinging
like a hammock, while metal detectors
scythe grass all afternoon.

Aerodynamic over paved trails,
the spandexed rollerbladers soar.
Under a muggy mix of cloud and sun,
even the rockroses undulate with poppies,
and tawny carpenters flash their zircon smiles,
hips holstered low with hammers
and locking retractable steel-tape measures.

One lonely cubit of lightning
coaxes roofers from aluminum ladders.
This is summer, perspicacious
as a paint scraper, steamy
as the skin's unstrung weather
of fine rain between the breasts.

Sing Cuccu, 4 a.m.

Sumer is icumen in,
Lhude sing cuccu!
            –British Library Harley 978

the clock speaks

The Pedantic talks
the fire to embers. Too much
espresso. The quick-

sand song of houseplants,
parched: Drip! Drip! Somewhere a car
starts. Snow tire studs click,

click pavement. Static:
polyester-blanket spark
spurs insomniac

downstairs. Her pen dips
and darts, it tries to trip its
shadow. Rocket launch

or syringe, inching.
What is there to say? Stylus
sniffs lonesome notebook.

The Romantics talk
this way: *Where have we . . . have we
met before?* Frisky,

flawless, paws licked and
stockings off, mattress ticking
upstairs. Not savage

exactly, these two,
but some prefer pas de deux
to the trombone's slide.

Outside, a clean script—
blizzard's cursive message etched
on moony snowdrifts.

Wary? Where am I
going with this late witness
[self-reflexive pause]?

It's a strange calling,
marking time, cuckoo, cuckoo,
head bobbing. Question:

If one could steam-bend
curves to swoop, to punctuate
the minute's sharp hand,

how might hours then
interrogate, or answer?
Whip-stitched minutes crimp

my yellowed face. My
arms wander. Furnace, stiff and
grumbling, turns over.

No beak's knitting nests,
twig by twig, yet. No birds of
a feather, ever.

Outside this described
circle, the hour bluing
its share of the sky,

the mice dart, hunting
crumbs from the kitchen table's
slice of pie. Warbling

north first, this compass
needle prowls toward warmth next,
striking east, southeast.

Alba Discotheque

winter sunrise

Pink-lamé sundogs
bodyguard
the bigwig's dazzled rise.
Steam gleams,
and billows blow
from a furnace vent
near the window
where ice hyphens wink,
crystallized and spun
beneath the molten
mirrored ball—
like sequined glitterati
or hungry paparazzi,
they flash
across a copper sky.

Downdraft

The deer dislike the lavender and heather.
Beyond the lattice fence, a buck browses
the youngest of the apple trees. The fig
swabs bedroom windows with its splashy leaves.
As if to hector the roses, pruned and mulched,
as if they've forgotten November, a scrawny pair
of poppies bristle and clench, too orange, too red:
thumbs in the eye of the weather. And a crow
plucks lumps of pumpkin from the compost bin.
I dry my boots beside the fire. I set
my tea to steep on the ledge. The dog's asleep
beneath my elbow. Warm as toast and snug,
smug as some tweedy squire, I survey
the possibilities. Who wouldn't stop
to watch those antlers strop? Who's never been
the thrashed sapling or brazen bud,
all thin dignity determined to arrive?
A gust pipes the chimney, chiff and fipple,
with a rasping hum, and a hum, and a downdraft
puffs once. Crow and pumpkin: yet to come.

January Walk

The wind has twisted the tops of hemlock and fir;
cones and needles spatter the muddy path.
Rising from nearby chimneys: woodsmoke and ash.
A cold mist washes my cheek, and cattails stir
the breeze, climbing dried and broken reeds,
while birdsong mixes swift, twitter, chit,
and sparrows hide among the rose-hip thickets.
My jacket snags on tangled arches, while beads
of dew fall from the vine. The year begins
anew. I thumb the cat-tongue underside
of a blackberry leaf, startled by its thorn.
One snapped branch divides our trail. The winds
have spun so little down. Despite the wide
weather warning, this time we missed the storm.

Cento: Note to Self

Tomorrow's tangle to the winds resign
And wash the dusk with silver soon, full soon
Announced by all the trumpets of the sky
The sea that bares her bosom to the moon

The ant's a centaur in his dragon world
The lowly worm climbs up a winding stair
And the lion glares through the dun forest
To lick his wounds in secret in his lair

How time has ticked a heaven round the stars
And lip to lip it murmured while you live
Little we see in Nature that is ours
Awake Aeolian lyre, awake, and give

LIKELY STORIES

Lullaby Postmodern

Meditation offers calm,
but I haven't an om in me.
Tempted instead
by drowsy clover,
I drift with
apricot apostles,
my weightless body lounging
among cypress trees
when the doorbell rings.
Perturbed sardines appear.
What about us, they demand,
the key unrolling the can.
One flops to the floor.
I jump to shut the door,
sop up an oily puddle
with a towel. A gerbil winks
from the closet. Just ignore him,
I tell myself, spinning the globe
toward a new destination, some place
sheltered by white noise—a beach,
waves memorizing a shore?
Just when I'm salty, quelled,
curled into a tide pool,
the clams spit at me.
Let us in. Let us into your vision.

Nostalgia Now

Life is short, she said, when it wasn't,
when what she meant was she'd have time to make
excuses. Desserts first, another cliché.
She takes a knife from a drawer, knowing it doesn't
mean; it cuts. Its blade reflects nothing.
Onions. Pared potatoes.
                          Her mind's thumbing
a ride now down the highway of then when agony
was all about love, or maybe money,
or being good enough. Funny, the past,
regrets petrified in pyroclastic
flows. Gestured incivilities in traffic.
Contempt: the scripts spit back to minimum-wage
telemarketers who'd only rung from cages,
whose trespass cooled a dinner plate?
                          Laughing
backward, isn't that what it's for? Nostalgia?
Not that she feels callous, looking astern.
There's time to muse, waiting for pathology
reports, or surgeons suturing certain
futures. And so, for now, she much prefers
her window seat. The time time straps
her down to nurse the baby in her lap,
and she sits still enough to learn the names of birds.

The Vellum Curtain

Lovely can be lonely: the seaside, the prairie.
Though you'd prefer the smirk of pain, mistakes
made: risky sex with drunks in bars,
bad tattoos—the riddled past we carry.
That lonely can be lovely is also true.
You threw a stone to cast a capillary
wave, to prick the surface of the lake.
Now, dismiss it as too beautiful for you.
Why is it you can't wait to read the scars?

Anniversary

Amid persimmons of permission,
amid the shimmer and immersion
among the chaperones of asphodel
from the meadow of the soul,
they sashayed the aisle, pledged
between Siva and Parvati, blessed
among the nodding Buddhas;
kinfolk wept through the sutras.
Wineskins freshened with sauvignons.
In filigree above, the violins. The violins
exalted them like diadems.
Passion played, teasing orchids.
And they coursed through ventricles
of cherish and reveal toward
the delta of promises. I will aurora
to your borealis, she said, wed,
and didn't. She did remember.

Long Division

With so much lost, they occupy the hours
with reinvention—taekwondo, new wardrobes,
flights of fancy—one lavish Eiffel Tower
trip before the assets split. Who'll comb
the yard sales, the beaches, the classifieds? Who'll keep
the majolica, the Sarouk, the house, its hush?
And how to split the photographs? Who'll speak
for none of it, start fresh with ferns or starfish
to trim the newly whitewashed walls? He bids
on love again. They haven't yet agreed
who'll get Thanksgiving or Christmas with the kids.
She feather-dusts the furniture and kneads
the bread dough with her fists. And if they'd tried
harder? She kept the dog, but the dog died.

Seed Catalog

Hoping perhaps to sweeten her up, he spoons
more honey in the tea. But no. *Chiuso.*
This church is closed for renovations. Ouzo?
It's too early. All morning, jackhammers tuning
up the street, scaring away business
from local shops and cafés. If only she'd jog,
pop vitamins. Where's that nuisance of a dog
when she needs him? Snatching a dish towel from the isthmus
of laundry, she snaps at the window. Damn deer
devour all her flowers. She keeps, she keeps
nattering on about the strewn petals,
her last murdered tulip. You've got to reap
what you sow, girl. Get a grip. Next year,
move the bulbs. Stung, plant nettles.

Bicoastal Arcana: Empress Inverted

She should have been more risk averse at thirty,
in her fricassee of pity, her smelt of hormones.
He shouldn't have left her quite so long alone
folding clothes. It wasn't enough, the thrifty
coin-op throb of the washer's spin cycles,
his vexing faith in her, secure as time zones.
And when he yawned on the telephone . . .
glittering from the balcony, icicles.

Swords? Wands? A slow thaw: a sign?
What if she wasn't *meant* to be neglected?
Now, how not to be? How to divine,
with a soupçon of self-respect, an exit
stage left? The last act would not be good.
She hadn't lied, yet, quite, but she knew she would.

Vespers

Valets to the sky,
these trees
hold a dinner jacket
high—sunset's cravat
thatches a throat
as evening glides
into its sleeves.
One star rappels
velvet heaven.
Another pierces a lapel—
the bleary boutonniere,
before it disappears,

before we wake
to the frost and air,
vanishing where
we'd wish to belong,
paroled outside
the lamplit homes'
berceuse hum,
the pledge of eternity's
idle song
that surfs and breaks
with the tide.

Hertzsprung-Russell

an astronomical diagram

The sky is a bouquet of old news.
Its gap-toothed vendor was Italian;
his roses unfurl galaxies.
From red to gold to blue,
From Barnard's Star to Rigel,
I plot the curve of magnitude.

Memory's a planetarium.
A twilit rustle, a sequin, an eye—
I squint to see a spectral class
of foxes cluster near the hedgerow.
Which luminosity is true?
That which is apparent
isn't absolute.

If history is a map of courage,
then the heart is made of helium.
This is a parallax to love:
you and I tilting sideways
with the surf, ordering
a string of stars inside the axis
of the plundered trees.

EPISTOLARY

Long Distances

With Qetesh

When vapors enamel the streets
after evening assaults of rain,
when the air ferments, June bugs
coupling high, black shine
beneath the streetlamp's beam,
and I scythe sheets, heat
holding back the tabernacle
of calming arms, then my mind ticks
awake, ready for exodus, ready to take you
from a summer sultry as uranium
to the vestibule of dreams
where I unravel you, slowly,
your tongue vermouth, sweeter than a wish,
sedition, forgive me this ventriloquy—

I would follow locusts to soak you
in a samovar large enough for both of us,
spigots bleeding out treacle and vinegar,
foaming us in phosphorus;
I would dab damp shadows
with ambergris, strum ligaments
with balms to dissolve grief
and bitterness, to gleam and polish
your exoskeleton, your silvery antennae,
your sheathed wings; and I would lead you
from hammam to temple where we would become
iridescent as scarabs, blessed as fetishes,
and then, my beetle,
then, my lustrous one . . .

With Dog

Dear Guillemot,
           Hello. I'm home from yoga.
Today: gull-gray, no news. Fergus pranced
the beach, stick jutting, left jowl, roguish.
His gait's a gloat: ever the handsome captain
chewing, puffing on his fat cigar.
We're here wondering how you are, so say
you're lonesome for us, even if you aren't.
Shopped. Swept. Mopped. Moped. Sigh.
I've come to know the summer by the ache
it brings, phone ringing me awake,
6 a.m., when, for the flutter of
a filmstrip, we're spliced sleepily together,
the distance snipped to cutting room litter.
To better weather, from the Rough of Love.

With Wherefore Art

Dear Montague,

Armchair-charming uncles
pucker close by;
dish-clatter and aunt-gabble
echo from an alcove
above the clack of cameras—
a flash for every mouthful.

Guess who burns for less
than this barbecued excess?
They're so bock and jolly,
but here, below my elbow,
pints of porter pour torpor.

You, sport, you're postage due,
and I'm sullen unless online,
typing lipstick lines on nylon.
Pity me—oh, my lion.
More amorous morass
tomorrow, Romeo.
Until then, I am,

Your Rapt Capulet

With Weathervane

What's missing?
The wind vanished.
The moon hasn't yet bloomed
in the sky. Night is timid
and stiff with stars.
The weathervane creaks,
but, steady servant,
holds east.
This copper veteran,
tarnished verdigris,
stays true as the buoy chiming
across the tide.
Rising now
and nearly fuchsia,
it's the languid poppy moon.
She'll soon become
a pollen-white chrysanthemum,
and coax this gloomy heart
to drum in time, in time,
as the temple thrums.
Watch set, no rest.
The pillow's timbrel tap-taps
this rainy song.
Absence reigns long here,
while my compass
shivers dawn.

With Camel

After the sweet trifles of salaam alaikum,
the verbal décolletage, the petal blizzard,
and smoke signals of smoldering frankincense
comes the long afternoon wobble
of one awaiting a reply. Sound travels farthest
along low frequencies, so say the elephants,
while, half a world away, the beloved yawns.
His shade is drawn.

Poor spent corsage of courage
and the crushed tissue of I miss you,
and the send-and-receive-all chronicle
of thought. No sputter. No zephyr.
No pulse. Dust settles implacably
atop the laptop's buttoned lip.

Collapse of Camelot? After moonrise, wife wonders,
tapping her thermometer. Ear to the ground
for the next low murmur, she hears what?
Dahlias hissing at the stars? A fingertip tracing
the wine glass rim of a clavicle? The amplified throb
of bedouins bedding? Hey, who's breathless by lamplight?

Whirling dervish whips into a sirocco
as sandstorms sting kohl-painted eyes—
anguish is aerobic, see? Like exercise.
En garde! She parries the hours,

twirling the tangled filigree of promises
around her finger. She tires of the swashbuckle.
Furtive in the abaya's black abyss,
she fetches her fletches, smooths her skirt,
sips a bromide, nibbles on a scone.

Meanwhile, morning lights the desert.
Sultan straightens his kaffiyeh,
mounts his camel once again,
waving cheerily toward home.

Letter to Santa

double-half-decaf abecedarian

A little tinsel, maybe? Sleigh bell jolly razzmatazz?
Bring it on: firelight, Santa's lap, spruce and holly.
Carols sung, *pa rum pa pum pum*. If I could just relax.
Deliver me from global worry—3 a.m. Plump my pillow?
Eggnog's empty. I'm prisoner of the wind, need a shiv
For my stocking. New camisole for my trousseau—
God, rouse my merry gentleman. What else is on my list?
Ho, ho, so glad you asked. Minimize the maximus,
if you would, of this gluteus. Sweet nothings murmur,
Jingle me, trim my tree. And this, Kris Kringle, Esq.,
kiss me? While I watch you unwrap?
Love me, Saint Nick. O,
much more mistletoe! Yours, again, with estrogen.

Rhymes

rho· do· den· dron

True forest archer, your arrow
airborne, the sky quivers (or do
I?) when it strikes home. Home: a den
of ferns and cedar boughs, the drone
of bee dances above, the pierced heart's pink blossom: rhododendron.

val· en· tine

Not serpentine, nor round as rings, love's oval
orbits as it sings. Ash fall: not yet, not again, Lent!
Here longing lasts, hear prayer that asks the spring to make me thine,
tic-toc, to quicken time, make thee mine, only Valentine.

HUMOURS

Choleric

at twenty

Life drawing. The figure model's attitude
is modest exhibitionist. Not bold
enough. More like the drapery, its folds
barely held, falling off the nude.
Still life: a kerosene lamp, smoking. A bowl
of daisies or a light switch without a rheostat.
Crepe paper, tearing. Rothko's splotches, abstract.
Music: blues would be too woozy; try zydeco.
The student cramming: sine or cosine?
Tangent: waitress, pinched, pours coffee, good
and hot, into that bastard's lap. Sharks
and minnows, with vertigo. Spun are the street signs
of my neighborhood. Where is the mother who would
sing my name from the back porch after dark?

Melancholic

at thirty

No dream sprung sullen from sleep's black comfort. No dream.
No story yet to wind around her hands.
A flank march across the temples, the lurch landing
of the stomach, the gasp. In extremis
a body tags truth first, its terrors all
corporeal; the mind's no match. And madness,
ethereal, escapes mass: an adjective
that shakes and slaps its noun. Crumbling, half-
gnawed, the moon's the bolus that every leaf
twitches toward. It beams. It pitches its pillbox
promise of equilibrium while belled
maidens poussette across the lawn. If she
ingests, amanita, your diminutive suffix,
will you carve for her a heart with gills?

Phlegmatic

at forty

Pursed lips: less than no, but not yet yes,
A whiff, more when than if, if often perplexed.
Veined maple leaf ablaze in a halting fall
and the sideways rain. The red tricycle,
white porch peeling paint, housebroken
dalmatian. Shutter-click witness with camera lens.
And sandpaper abrading the surface of the day,
although I didn't mean to grow old this way.
And when did my "O" become a yawn? One eye
closed evades the moon's white glow. I
have become the desk, plagued, the bed, made.
The ship's bell on the bronze lamp, its red-drum shade.
So many postures I can't maintain. The stave.
The fountain pen inked before it engraves.

Sanguine

at fifty

If life is an open vein, then what's brave
about a sleeve heart, sweetheart? Up's so often
up against, a slave to passion and outrage, uncaged,
fed fat as a harbor seal watching the locks.
Life has its ups and downs. I feel, I feel,
fish meal. Am I bleeding again? One grows tired,
second-guessing, when yes can't help but acquiesce.
The sky is still the sky. Once in a monsoon,
your schooner blew in, and hope faceted
like a deck prism. Someone chloroformed the oracles.
Since then, cloud-wise, we ride the seas and swells fairly well,
fleet as leeches, I'd say. It takes a sheet wound round the winch
to tourniquet the pulse, to slow the thrum. Rumor has it,
I'm steadying, my love. Maybe I'll quiet down.

Humours Remix

Bronze lamp, ship's bell.
We ride the seas and swells.

If madness is ethereal
then chloroform the oracle.

The rheostat. The Rothko, splotched.
A harbor seal watches the locks.

The smoking lamp. The model bolder.
I didn't mean to grow older.

CRYPTOPORTICO

Finger Exercises

i.

Rough bristles buff tough tufa bright
to smear the moon on square and street.
In orange jumpsuits workers sweep,
and bottles scrape the Roman night.
A hush floods as the sky grows light,
when weary travelers slump, asleep.

ii.

Bleary tourist orders double
jet-lag stalling macchiato,
pays for peaches, steps staccato
off to gawk at ancient rubble.

iii.

The umbrellas collapse
when the market breaks down.
Watch the gulls and the swifts
as they circle and sift
through the lost and found
of trashed napkins and maps.
If a mind in its flight
could swoop low now and then,
pluck from life's souvenirs
one bright wrapper, the gift
of a light bob to fix
to the tail of its kite,
never roosting on fear
before lifting again . . .

Doth the Same Tale Repeat

Café. Sketchbook. Sun
marbling the green leaves
of this umbrella. Wristwatch:
tic, toc—what's time
to the tourist—idle scribbler
sipping cappuccino,
setting down the lost capital,
the lichen-covered colonnades
that kiss the sky? Why,
fountain warbler, pigeon chaser,
cheese taster, do you follow the cobbles
with your thundering suitcase,
do you peer through the light
of the only golden plum?
Wipe that coffee stain
from your laminated *mappamondo*.
You, with the colossal plan,
get that gladiator down:
gilded helmet, red-plumed costume,
cupped hand—whom does he woo
with his cell phone chitchat?
Shake off the sadness
of that broken sandal strap.
The sky is bigger than the oculus.
Seeking shade in cryptoporticus,
sweaty in the ruins of some igneous villa,
do you envy ash? Millennia

in the Hall of Mysteries' rich red rooms?
What word in your volcano could resist
erasure? And who shall measure?
A breeze teases a candle
as the phrase book falls from the table,
riffling from tarot to *tesoro mio:*
sorrow's treasure.

Triads

In the Garden

Spare rib—
Adam's apple
Evening.

Wet

Early Sunday rain on the Campo.
The parasol and the penitent.
Tears underneath umbrellas.

Half

Limping pigeon in the Pincio.
Conversation under cathedral bells.
Mascara-smeared stranger, face eclipsed by one hand.

A Cavallini Annunciation

fresco fragments, Santa Cecilia in Trastevere

One angel lunges forward,
arm raised. Two fingers bless
the Virgin, seated on a throne.

Remnants of a red cross
lost somewhere behind her—
fresco keeps falling off of stone.

No stalk left with lilies blooming,
no dove
arcing like a meteor above.

The hands float.
One holds her robe;
one rises to the chest, palm facing in.

What else erased?
Her face
shows no fear, no surrender, no repose.

Notes from the Etruscan Necropolis

the Villa Giulia

I am Scuria's jar.

My words speak right to left in long, thin letters.

Trace my aristocracy through my mother's lines.

I refer only to my donor,
followed by the name of my worshipped god.

I may be a liver or a uterus.
I contain the universe.

In my tongue there is no epigraphic evidence
of the word for king.

In the partition of the vault of heaven, for instance,
the propitious divinities reside on the eastern side.

You there, nodding off in your wicker chair
near the air conditioning vent:
do you feel the limes dropping behind you?

I am of Lupe Thernicina of Fulu (who is dead).
Don't steal me.

Met·a·mor·pho·sis

Apollo, arrow struck, thinks he's met
the one lithe, lovely maiden meant for him. A
god's got no worries. What's one more chase? More amor!
Daphne, Daddy's girl, thinks maybe she'll become a nun. Fuss
follows, laurel leaking from fingertips. Barking up the wrong tree, that's what this is.

The Archaic Torso of Apollo

freely after Rilke

This guy's lost his head but, Jesus,
what radiance gleams beneath the pectorals,
and, as the eye follows the contours
south toward genesis, well,
one could go blind smiling.

Sure, the surface is stone, chipped
here and there, but who wouldn't be taken
by those shoulders, and underneath,
can't you see the blaze? A star
goes nova inside you. You can't hide
anymore. You must get a life.

Odalisque, Titian's Bacchanal

Her elbow high, her auburn locks long
and drizzled down her spine, Ariadne
arches. She's draped at the shoulders only,
and dreaming holy raptures—or am I wrong?
Blink twice. How does one tell heaven from steam?
A question worth pursuing someday, but
the revelers don't care, and every other
nubile maid engages eyes while sleeves
cascade down arms. Pitchers salute the sky,
the wine half gone. Yet she prefers to pose
for some lone fantasy of love, not raise
a glass. *Foolish, foolish,* shrieks the presiding
guinea hen from her tree, and the god dozes,
legs splayed across a green hill far away.

Postcards from Ponza, the Prison Island

1.

My panoramic lens apprehends
a hammock slung between two lemon trees.
Beyond the terra-cotta potted palms,
grapes cluster, plump slubs twisting
through the vineyard's unwound skeins. Damp towels
flap in the hibiscus-heavy breeze,
and terraced hillsides ziggurat to meet
a rocky harbor. Splashed coral pink
and periwinkle blue, flat-roofed villas,
like licked stamps, attach and overlap
around a sprawling beryl bay.

2.

Tacking in and out of view, a yawl
runs and comes about, heeling over
the old caldera. A guidebook tells me
it's Pontius Pilate (so legend has it) for whom
the island's named. He bellows from a grotto.
And Circe taunts the seas. Hear her laugh
above her snorting, truffle-hunting crew?
Expats conspire beside me. I spy, maybe,
the plotting sisters of Caligula,
exiled here eternally. What luck
to spear an olive with such dauntless ghosts.

3.
Swollen Zodiacs weave water webs
across a shallow cove—wakes froth
from yacht to jetty to wobbling dock—
throttled down, they set their bowlines now,
looping cleats, tying up. One slip over,
a trawler unloads the day's cargo. The catch:
slick holds of *polpi* and scampi, soon to swim
the length of a rich *risotto pescatore.*

4.
Toasting Monte Guardia, I raise
my rubied glass past fifty fish eyes staring
from a basket. Did I seize the day?
Did I mention yet the always amber light?
I plot to overthrow the god that shrimps
my shoulders. Even here, I know, I'm not
Gina Lollobrigida. Not yet.

5.
Gina Lollobrigida I'm not.
So what? We just got here. Our pensione?
It's lovely, only the bedroom door won't lock.
And what have we to steal, my beloved asks?
I feel it too, but, to be safe, standing
on the countertop, I reach three shelves
above our kitchenette to stuff the passports
in a stoneware crock. I don't unpack. I do
refold a suitcase full of clothes, ever
ready for departure.

6.

                    Did you see her,
back there, the one who just whizzed past, straddling
the Vespa, spackled across the trapezius
of his (whose?) brawny torso? A carabiner
clipped her bikini to a haversack;
it slapped the sky.

7.

                  I set a cosmetic case
beside the mirror. Bottled serums clink
against vials of embalming oils.
How much happiness is squandered waiting
for the end? The present tenses when
it can't accommodate the future. And we
just got here. Madame Pluperfect peeps
through her marcasite lorgnette. Above
her head, contrails swipe and pig the firmament.

WINGED ELBOW

First Chantey

From tumbled starshine
once upon a time
and the stethoscope's echo,
calendar pages punched confetti,
from the submarine jelly-roll
periscope view into
mare nostrum's water ballet,
from the caged sashay
of a winged elbow
from the dark swan dive,
fists first squinting
at the surface glare,
from the close-reefed sails
in a broad reach,
and the wind's red wail relenting,
to you,
becalmed at last, latched
at the mooring of a milky sea.

Matin

In my dream I am lost, but this is not
a dream about being lost, and the house
which is my house does not accumulate
unknown corridors or secret rooms.

All summer I've been drawing plans, making
a cottage in my mind, without stairs,
sidled against a maple wood, facing
fields and ridge lines we'll have no need to climb.

In the night, when I rise to answer the owls,
I am guided by familiar walls, feeling
my way through the known dark, careful not
to wake my beloved or our sleeping child.

Let these be: the beloved, the child, and always
in my house and my dream. May I find
the kitchen's east windows where the sky
and the clock foretell again a future of mornings.

A kettle calls to the earliest warblers, while
the bats return to rest along the eaves.

The Fairy Tale

Mind of water in the wet winter,
bemused mother watches for crows
from her perch at the keyhole window.
She minds a daughter, a minister to morning,
who grows cold with her bowl of millet,
hailing seed onto bark. She hopes to catch
a hopping junco or grackle or flicker
or wren. She gleams in the rain,
peering beyond the unlatched garden gate,
and waits to pounce—a feathery chase,
and a vanishing choreography of birds.

Sweep the pine needles into a heap,
she says, *few by few.* Hands warming,
she charms even the andirons, chanting:
Fire, fire, blaze bright! Flames leap
to the sky! But don't burn down the house,
whimpers the whisperer, reason.
Sea of my heart, she sprays
the waves' flowers over me—*Lucky life.*
Why must I pivot, hover, check
behind, expect the sudden shoulder slap,
the trap, the jackal, treason.
Canary cough. Capsized cradle.
Make me over as a moss ledge
in the trickle of time.
Chirp. Alight on the bough.
Sing, house finch.

Laundry Tokens

Colloidal Suspension

June: dingy, stained gray.
Housewife searched sky all day for
bluing solution.

Ironing Board

Rumpled thoughts flattened
over asbestos cover
press into ideas.
Clean linen steams, stretched until
legs screech, collapsing.

Finding

Red glass bead
tumbles from a pocket.
A holographic locket?
Whose palmed charm
mimics, chimes alarm?
To be fused, not freed—
one petrified petal
raps against metal.

Antoinette

One tuna sandwich locked in the lunch box,
the child is breakfasted, dressed, and brushed.
After, the blown kiss at the school bus,
a trailside jog with the dog, chasing ducks.
Shower. Yoga stretch. A glimpse of sun.
Fingering, badly, a forgotten étude
on the piano, newly tuned.
Flapping like a grackle over gravel
midmorning to the mailbox,
checking for checks.
How can I sit here, like this,
flaunting happiness?
I haven't even assembled
the tsunami emergency kit.
The French press brews.
I don't choose to read the news;
something's always bound to get us.
Steady rain on the skylight tries to drip in.
Meanwhile, the unruptured soap bubble
in which I and the tooth fairy still coexist.
Let the debt ceiling wait. Let them eat cupcakes.

The Story Problem

I won't let them in the house.
The endocrine disruptors.
The child soldiers.
My daughter's pressed clover
slips from her math book into my lap.

Jehovah's Witnesses ring the bell.
Dressed for success,
they'd smile through the apocalypse.
Such is the gift of a god's love.
They leave me with leaflets.

I won't let them in the house.
Families huddle in rock caves,
thinking small.
All day shells fall
on the Sudan. Such is the gift of government.

The forecast for Syrian neighborhoods?
Aerial bombardment. The wind swarms,
and the house quakes.
I lie awake.
In Wyoming, fracking decocts a well.

The reach of waves amazes me.
Winds swarm and houses quake.
Bits of plastic wash up on the beach.

Power is cheap.
Cesium percolates from breached tanks.

Describe the half-life of a hot particle.
How many cancers can dance
on the head of a pancreas?
Story problems:
a few to add to the algebra books.

Describe the half-life of a news article.
A lipless woman with half a face
makes her escape. The story problem
slips into my lap. I lie awake,
thinking small.

In Sæcula Sæculorum

There is no end of beauty.
Paperweights can't pin its pages down.
Even as we deny it, we try to hold it nearer.
Shoulder blades ache in the dark.
One arm drapes across a small body
breathing, laughing in sleep.

Have we become too frail for joy,
our fear too fierce for the raptures
that pierce saints or kindle children?
If not joy, we say, then peace:
to be content with absence,
to dispossess, to contain nothing.

Why am I a vessel then?
To feel is to fill and to fall.
We profess disinterest,
as if pain were punishment.
We girdle the garden
with disquisition. We expel ourselves.

Each morning before dawn strains,
birds sing. Each spring the wedged buds burst
in rain, and violets buffet the grassy hillsides.
And later, the owl's steady, dusk-lit call.
And then, the surprised cry and struggle
of a hunted animal. Beauty begets agony.

We are scarred. The rabbi nods.
So, we are scarred. Memory sears us,
and we scorn loveliness.
We are not starved. We are not sieves.
Bereft of what we once loved well,
we remain vain, vanishing.

Where caution pinches us we retract.
Lurking in penumbra, lacking
the courage to reflect the sun,
we wane. Brittle with wishes,
we are rich as dragons,
while billboards blaze
the end of days.

VICOLO

No amount of scepticism and criticism has yet enabled me to regard dreams as negligible occurrences. Often enough they appear senseless, but it is obviously we who lack the sense and ingenuity to read the enigmatic message from the nocturnal realm of the psyche.

Carl Jung

Call on God, but row away from the rocks.

Indian Proverb

Vicolo del Divino Amore

What's to be made of it? *Divine love,*
when God's touch torch-lit Adam's fingertip?
When the winged one pressing lilies to his lips
hushed the girl, and pulled the white dove
from God's magic hat? One summer in Rome,
needing to be forgiven and faltering,
I lit the candles beside the gold-leafed altars
and knelt, a penitent under every dome.
I bowed to a Virgin I, no Catholic,
couldn't know. I willed to believe and made
promises. So when my belly flowered
with the future, and my one wish kicked
and stitched herself into the world, I prayed
my gratitude. Grace: an opened doorway.

Grace—la Madonna gravida within
her quiet garden, glinting marigolds.
A mercy born of myth and miracle—
a daughter. I dot the "i" of intercession,
chastened to learn so late that birth can lend
a chance to touch the hand of God. What God?
I grind a lens to see. The glass fogs
again beneath my breath. What token sent
me back to stalk along these chapel aisles?
No trance-led sibyl's cherry-laurel murmuring
among the fumaroles. A coin thrust
into a box, a switch flipped. The niche's dial
timer ticking—*luce!* For one alluring
moment, the artifice of painting brushed

a heart. Ambush. What art begets—a painted
faith. Cracked frescoes' fallen plaster pieced
together by the mind, I read the stories
of the eyes in each annunciation.
I study postures, gestures, faces, wrists.
Her dropped book. Her moment of surprise—
illumination. A patient hand applies
the pigments: lapis, cinnabar. With fists
full of pocket change, one lapsed agnostic
slinks cat-like beneath the coffers, evading
summer's scorch. The painting breathes. The dog-eared
guidebook doesn't mention this. Exhausted
tourist expects *aperitivo,* fated
to stumble once inside the vault. Steered

and tumbling, inside the vault, the mind begins
to do what minds can do—add and subtract:
The crowd. The heat. Thirst. Fatigue. An abacus
of explanations stacking beads against
the swoon of mystery. Flint-struck, the heart's
protective foil wrapper crinkles back;
the chest swells, throbbing like a maniac.
And then it's gone. The lime plaster hardens.
Buona giornata. What's true? What counts? A child
was born—unalloyed joy! It should have been
enough to shake me into faith and hold
me there. But I slept. I wandered. Heaven smiled,
and I veered away. Why? The light dimmed.
Not every angel's halo is gessoed gold.

Not every angel's halo is gessoed gold.
I trace a life—quill toppling the inkwell,
spilling east and west, midwife to a swell
of words delivered by the wind, a threshold
sweeper sifting for treasure on patrol.
At night, sometimes, when I forget
to breathe, asleep, I find myself—some aspect
of myself—caught between the depths and shoals
of dream and reason. When the tide is calm,
I preach the gospel of observation. The frontier!
Make me permeability's attaché.
The scrim lifts. I open my notebook. Psalms
scatter. Is this the way? Myopic seer
fletches fear. The way back? I shouldn't stay.

Why fear? I can't say, but fathom danger.
Who haunts the slope of slumber—sylph or cipher?
Talons seize a shoulder. *Be gone Lucifer!*
Then I remember—*Breathe!* One damaged angel
whumps away. A bright moon glares and mocks
me as I comb the ecliptic path for Mars
and Jupiter, my muscle men, my starlit
worry beads. Two. Three. Four o'clock.
Vexed at night's nexus, my mind checks dead bolts
and gas valves. I fence the distance from here to ether
with razor wire. Bad dream? Or was it more?
The truth smolders—I was in a dim cold
where soldiers crouched around the fire of a nether
world. Tighten my tether to this shore.

Tighten my tether. What was it? Not
divine—a visit out of time's dominion.
Steadied by the chimes that signal morning,
I shower it away. Wick-lit, a knot
of sun ignites the lantern world. I wear
the mantle of the day. I drink my tea.
The Ouija realm recedes to an idea,
an afternote of bergamot. Here
is Earth, a planet spinning in the sky
and the ground beneath my feet. The truth is,
the truth is elusive. My body bows and breathes.
Namaste. The dead stay dead. Why,
then, these confusing interviews? The sutra
says, *Outside the walls they stand.* Hungry,

these thieves of sleep. *Outside the walls.* Hungry
shades? I shrink from the thought. The woo-woo world
peers in. And what of those without walls, hurled
across that precipice, heeding lunacy's
alluring alto, or waylaid, non compos mentis
at the punch bowl, sipping a doctor's cocktail
for psychoses? Addicts stagger and flail.
We pass the narcotic sprawl, the self-contempt,
and turn away. Or leer from our own houses
at lap dancing spasms of the damned: the dark
circles, gone looks—*hungry shades*—dazed smiles.
How can one be indifferent or aroused?
The body clamps and cringes, though it sparks
inside, and haunches brush the fence. Denial:

the fence is brushed, the tail swishes. What's animal
then and what's divine? A torso flames
and opens, sacrum to crown. The moan became
the om, climbing the coiling column, lamina
lucida, flushed with heat, back arching
in sacramental bliss. What's love but God's
liminal valentine? The soul applauds,
the body's bell resonates—the tone marching
from toe to ear, from lip to fingertip.
And we are safe in the beloved's arms,
to go beyond, where pleasure knows no peril,
where all is easy alchemy, hip to hip.
No fall from paradise. The carnal charm—
when flesh, blessed, spent, rung, still peals the carillon.

Flesh blessed and rung. When I was young, my voice
changed once, mid-hymn, while I sang in church. So pure
were the notes, I knew they weren't mine, and sure
that this was God, I felt my throat, an oyster,
unhinged to reveal its pearl. So it seemed.
Years later, another pearl? Was it a cloud
that glittered its way to enter my neck. How?
A key? A slit gill or ripped seam?
It filled me. I shimmered, buoyant, opalescent,
and floated free, but wouldn't trust it. So,
I grew worried and willed myself awake.
I woke, or thought I did. The strange pageant
had barely begun—a goddess winking at the window,
A brace of racing hounds. Not there. My mistake.

Not there. Not awake, not yet. I tried to shake
it off, come up for air, open my eyes,
and still the dream kept reeling its surprises.
And when at last I found a way to break
the spell, I cried and couldn't sleep again.
Slipping into a posture of erasure,
I am an inmate, not a messenger.
What can it mean? Can't you make it plain?
The dead have things to say: *Have you lost your only*
mind? My grandmother assesses my divorce.
Don't let her go there, a sister warns me when
my daughter isn't safe. And they look lonely,
sometimes. My father, beside the fire. Remorse
is mine. So, did I seek them out? Night watchmen . . .

What did I seek? Who watches me? I may
believe the recently departed linger
and see us hunched in grief, straining to hear
the words of farewell whispered on their way.
A tender membrane opens for a moment.
How to account for nightmare visits from
one unbeloved—a soul I hadn't summoned
and couldn't know had died, after twenty
years and a thousand miles? In each dream room
I dodge and stammer, determined to conceal
my life from him. At least he hadn't
touched me. Why so afraid? A plume
of smoke quelled, dispelled by morning—not real—
just a dream. But I wake gasping, maddened

by just a dream. And what is it to dream,
when not so long ago we slept in trees,
and big cats prowled the ferns below? No breeze—
that tingle at the neck. Electric lemur
brain adrenalized to flee or fight.
The enemy's invisible and draws
no sword. And yet I feel the unsheathed claws
scraping bark. So now, how does one quiet
the mind, when reason's weakest in the dark?
I breathe. I hum a lullaby. I pay
a call on God to borrow just one angel,
the Botticelli model, please, to guard
my back, to hold my heart, to hear me pray:
oh spangled gods or muses, as I dangle,

tangled in these silken filaments,
I do wonder how much any artist
chooses. Is this a trap or lifeline? Startled,
the envoy of uncertainties repents.
The savant asks, do I spin, or am
I caught? I ought to know by now. Why do
I blink when the blindfold slips? And quickly stoop
to tie it on again? In the concave clamor
of a fast, I remembered grace, the doorway
opening. I considered the garden beyond,
the flame flicker within, the child, the chime,
the hail of voices rising above the roaring
nebula of glimmering souls at dawn,
"Once upon"—not yet! It isn't time.

The Drifting Envoi

I remember grace, the doorway,
the wish that flowered with the future.
I pay a call on God to borrow
the dial timer's ticking *luce*.
What do I seek? Who watches me
slink cat-like beneath the coffers?
Am I inmate? What can it mean?
The heart's protective foil wrapper
unhinges to reveal its pearl.
Psalms scatter. Is this the way
to go beyond, yet know no peril?
One damaged angel whumps away.
Across the precipice, hurled,
the sun ignites the lantern world.

Carol Light received the Robert H. Winner award from the Poetry Society of America in 2013 and an award from Artist Trust in 2012. Her poems have appeared in *Poetry Northwest, Narrative Magazine, American Life in Poetry, 32 Poems,* and elsewhere. She studied poetry in the University of Washington MFA program, where she was awarded the Academy of American Poets Prize.  She lives with her family in Port Townsend, Washington.

Heaven from Steam was a finalist for the 2012 Able Muse Book Award.

CPSIA information can be obtained
at www.ICGtesting.com
Printed in the USA
JSHW021928130123
36244JS00003B/143